M.D. LaBelle

Paintings and Drawings

FRONT COVER:

Bright Colored Flowers, 1995

Oil Pastel Stick on Paper

BACK COVER:

M.D. LaBelle, Michigan 2020

Black and White Photograph

Page 9:

Red Bird, 2021

Oil Pastel Stick on Paper

Page 10:

Bright Colored Flowers, 1995

Oil Pastel Stick on Paper

Page 11:

I See You, 1995

Charcoal on Paper

Page 12:

Violin, 1993

Pencil on Paper

Page 13:

No Face, 1994

Charcoal on Pape

Page 14:

Hummingbird, 1993

Pencil on Paper

Page 15:

Serious, 2020

Pencil on Paper

Page 16:

Faraway, 2019

Pencil on Paper

Page 17:

Christmas Time, 2020

Pencil on Paper

Page 18:

Fern, 1996

Graphite on Paper

Page 19:

Skelly, 1994

Pencil on Paper

Page 20:

Old Timer, 1992

Pencil on Paper

Page 21:

Ostrich, 1992

Pencil on Paper

Page 22:

Waterfall, 1993

Acrylic Paint on Canvas

Page 23:

Silence, 1995

Acrylic Paint on Canvas

Page 24:

Red Mountains, 1996

Acrylic Paint on Canvas

Page 25:

Blue, 1996

Acrylic Paint on Canvas

Page 26:

King Neptune, 1993

Wall Mural Paint

Page 27:

Serene, 1992

Watercolor Paint on Canvas

Page 28:

Outback, 1992

Watercolor Paint on Canvas

Page 29:

The Swan, 1991

Watercolor Paint on Canvas

Page 30:

Orange Lady, 1996

Oil Pastel Stick on Paper

Page 31:

Yellow Woman, 1996

Oil Pastel Stick on Paper

Page 32:

Red Lady, 1995

Oil Pastel Stick on Paper

Page 33:

Sitting Woman, 1995

Charcoal on Paper

Page 34:

Sitting Man, 1995

Charcoal on Paper

Page 35:

Laying Woman, 1994

Charcoal on Paper

Page 36:

Man Contemplating, 1995

Graphite Stick on Paper

Page 37:

Man Laying, 1994

Charcoal on Paper

Page 38:

About the Artist

Page 39:

Copyright Page

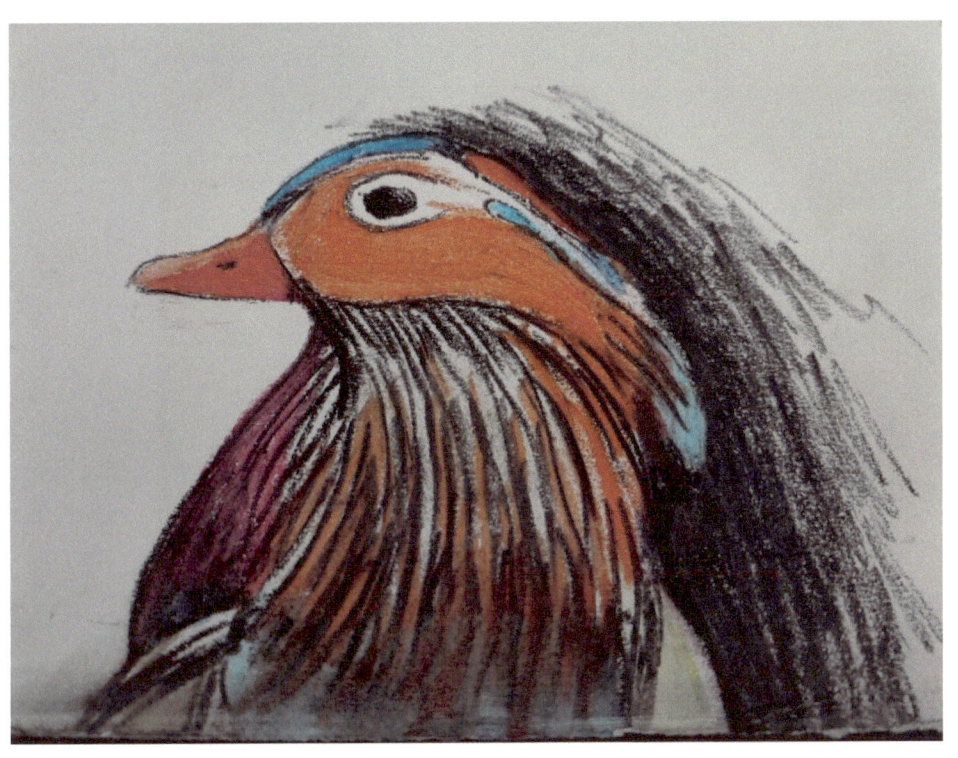

Red Bird, 2021

Oil Pastel Stick on Paper

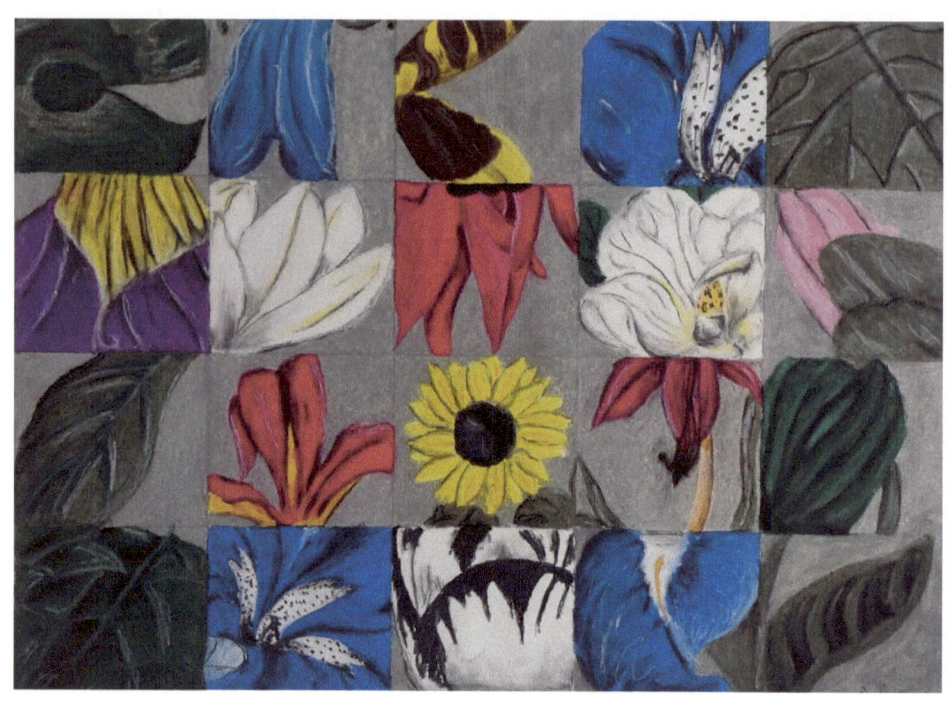

Bright Colored Flowers, 1995

Oil Pastel Stick on Paper

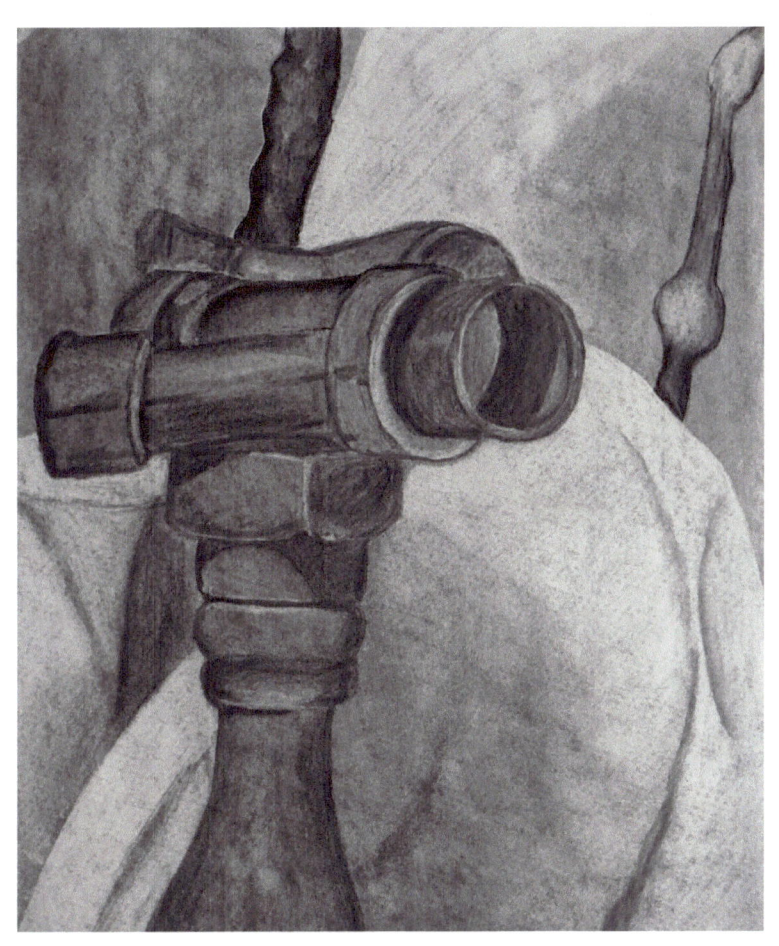

I See You, 1995

Charcoal on Paper

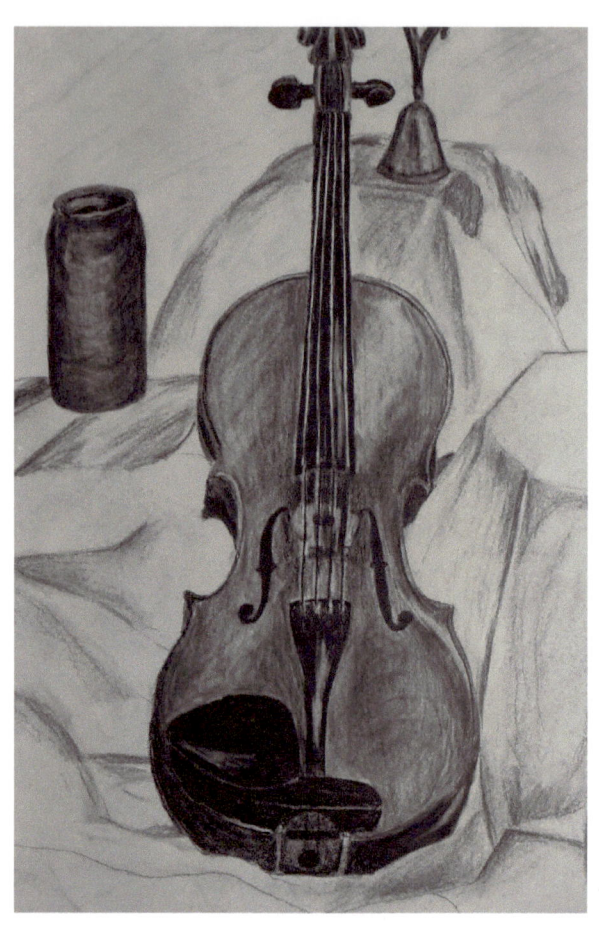

Violin, 1993

Pencil on Paper

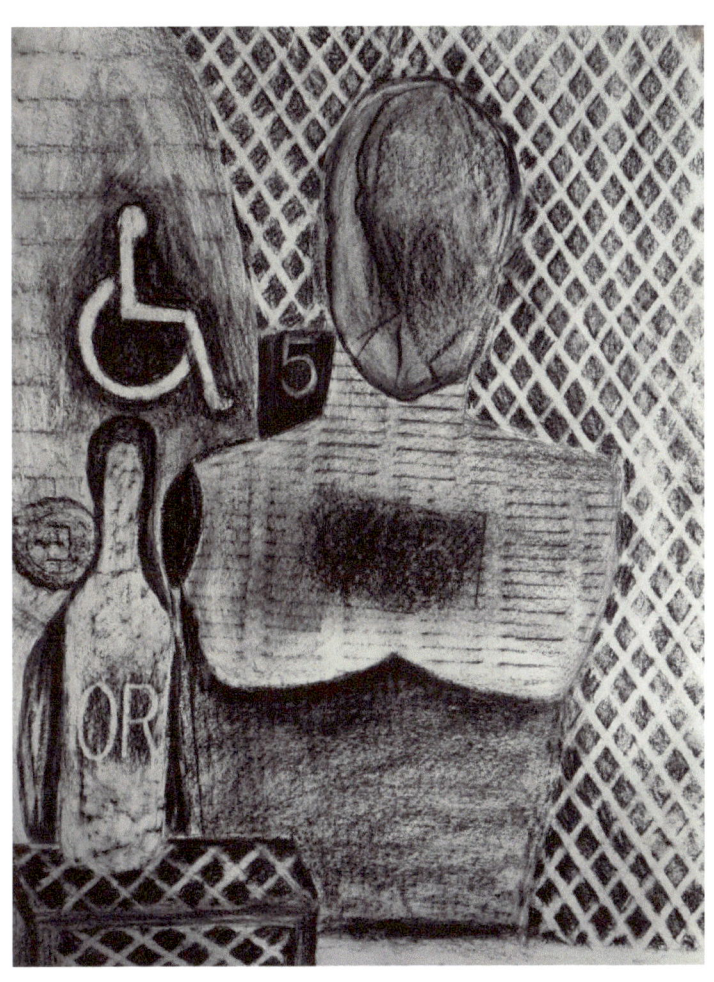

No Face, 1994

Charcoal on Paper

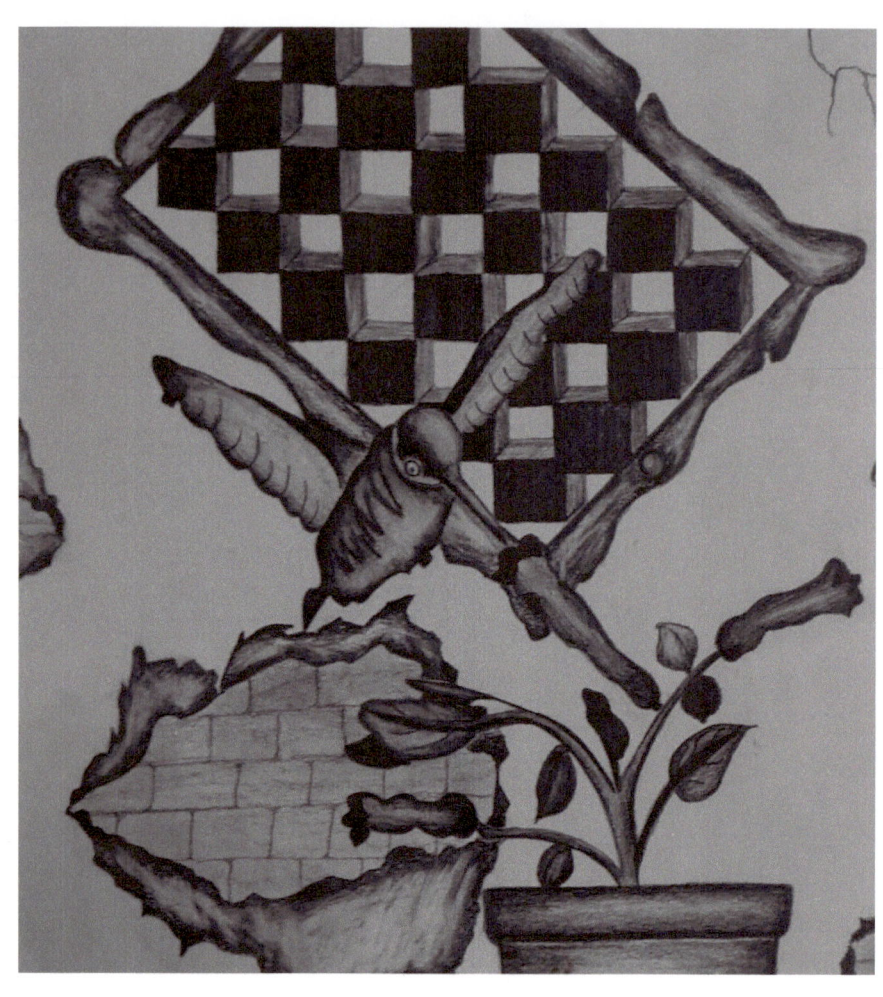

Hummingbird, 1993

Pencil on Paper

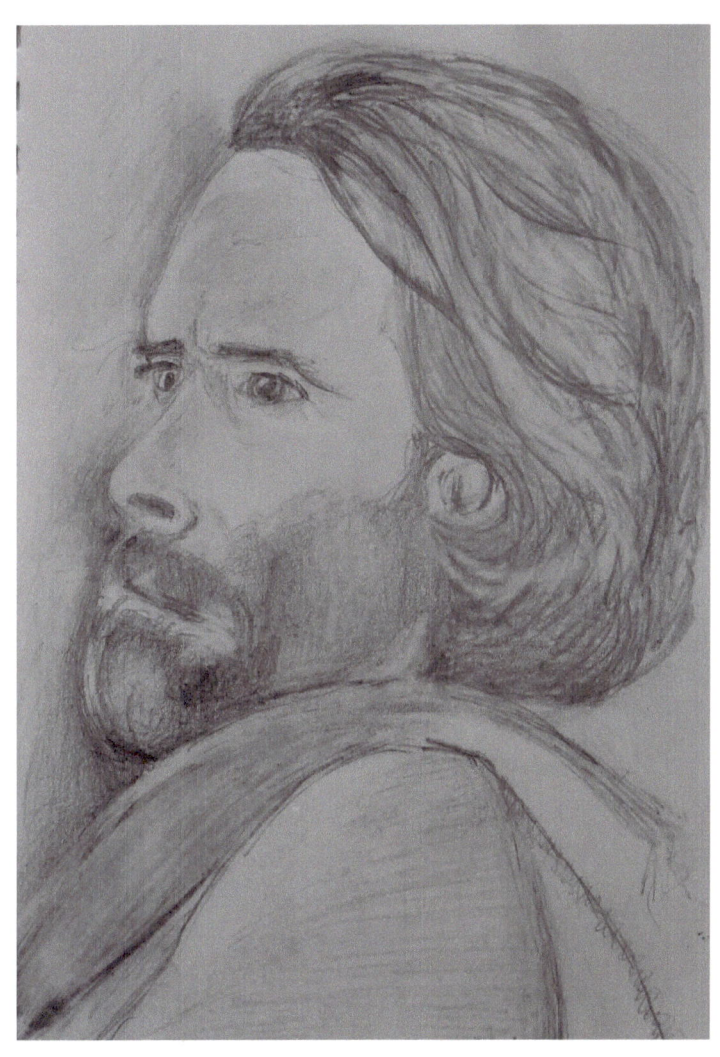

Serious, 2020

Pencil on Paper

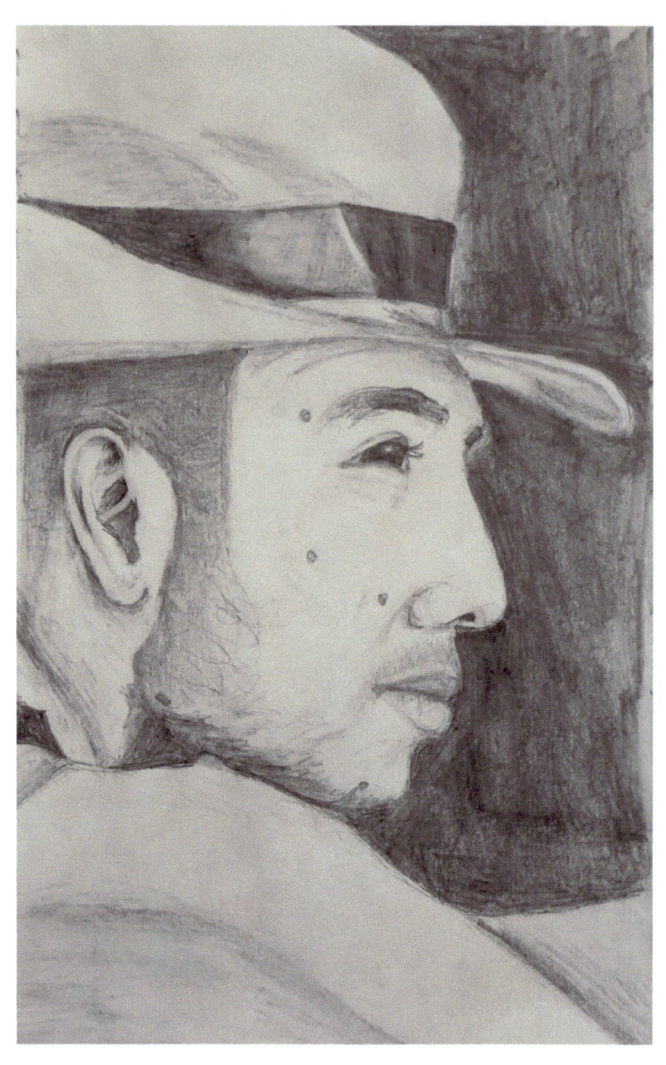

Faraway, 2019

Pencil on Paper

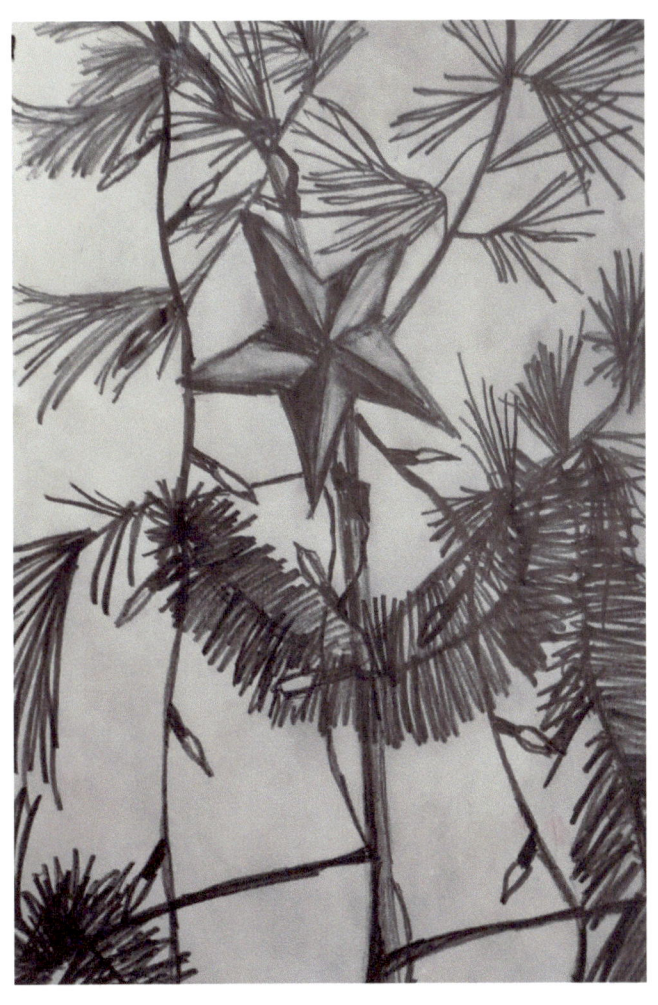

Christmas Time, 2020

Pencil on Paper

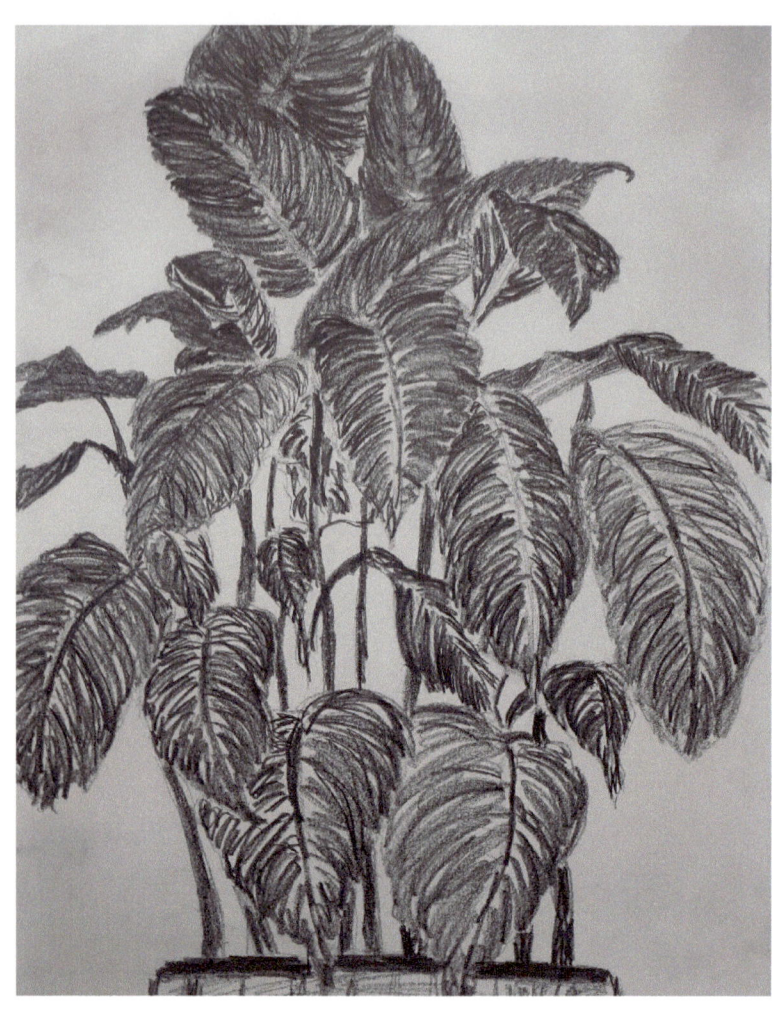

Fern, 1996

Graphite on Paper

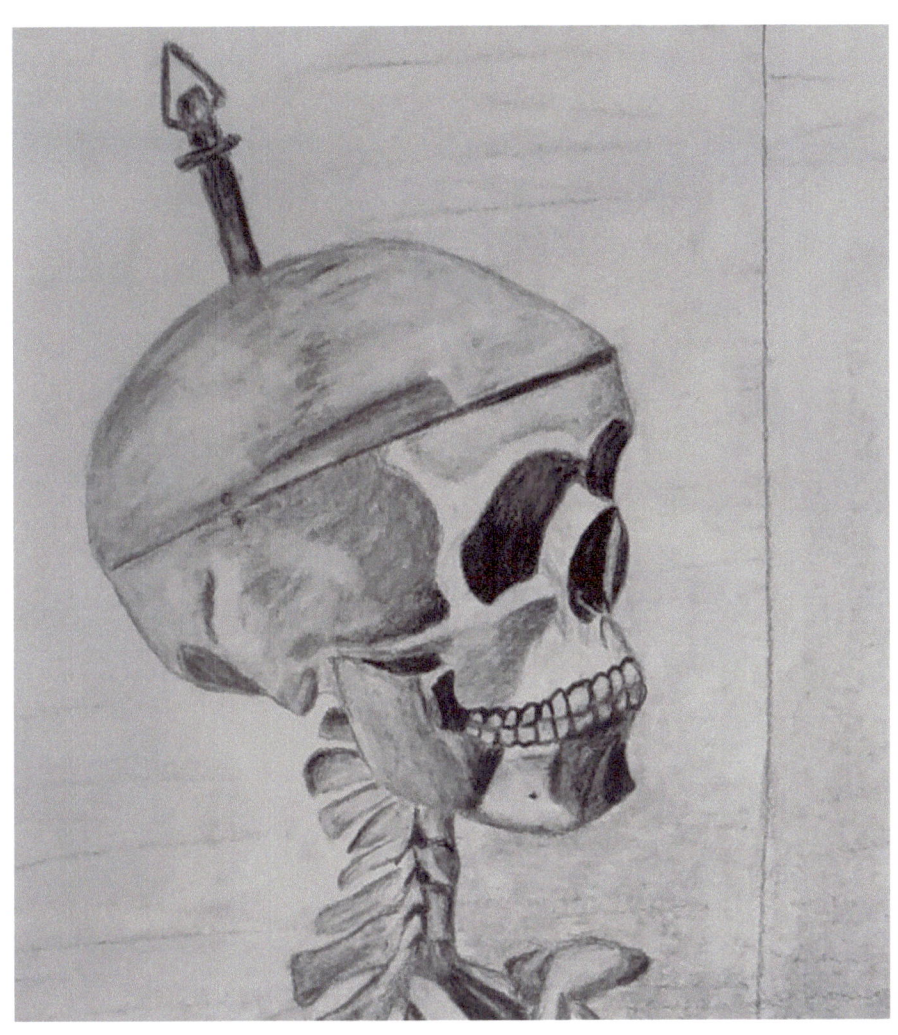

Skelly, 1994

Pencil on Paper

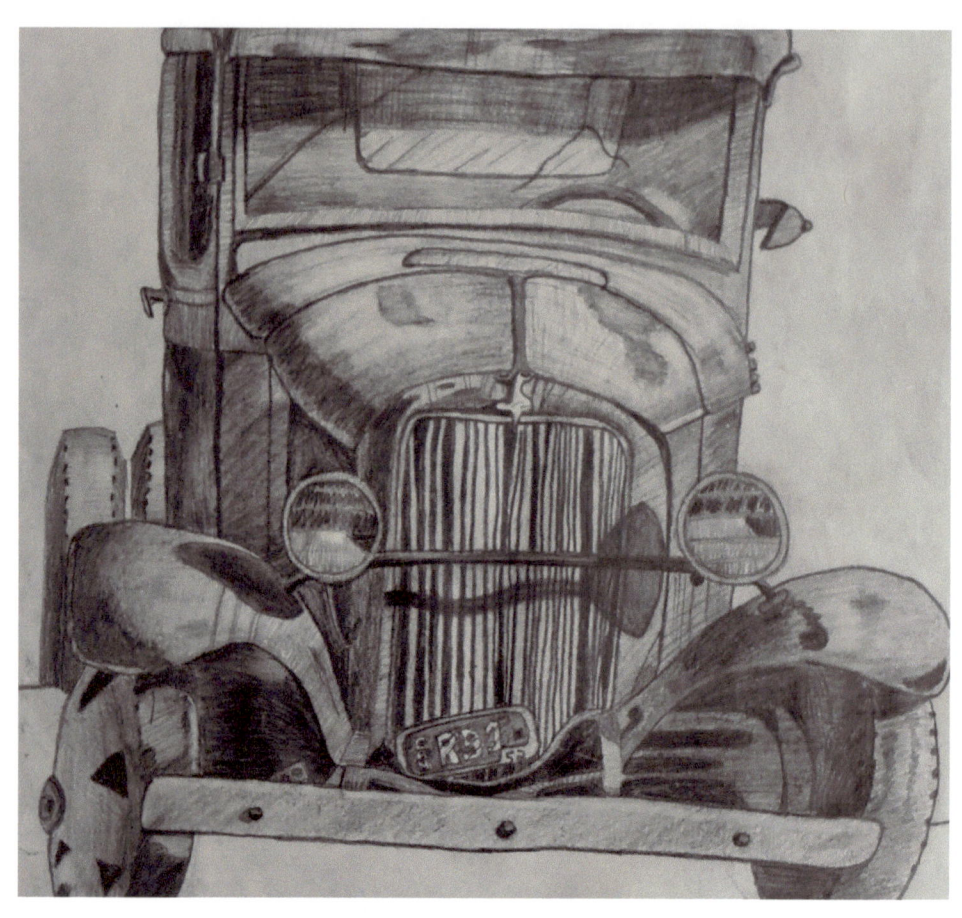

Old Timer, 1992

Pencil on Paper

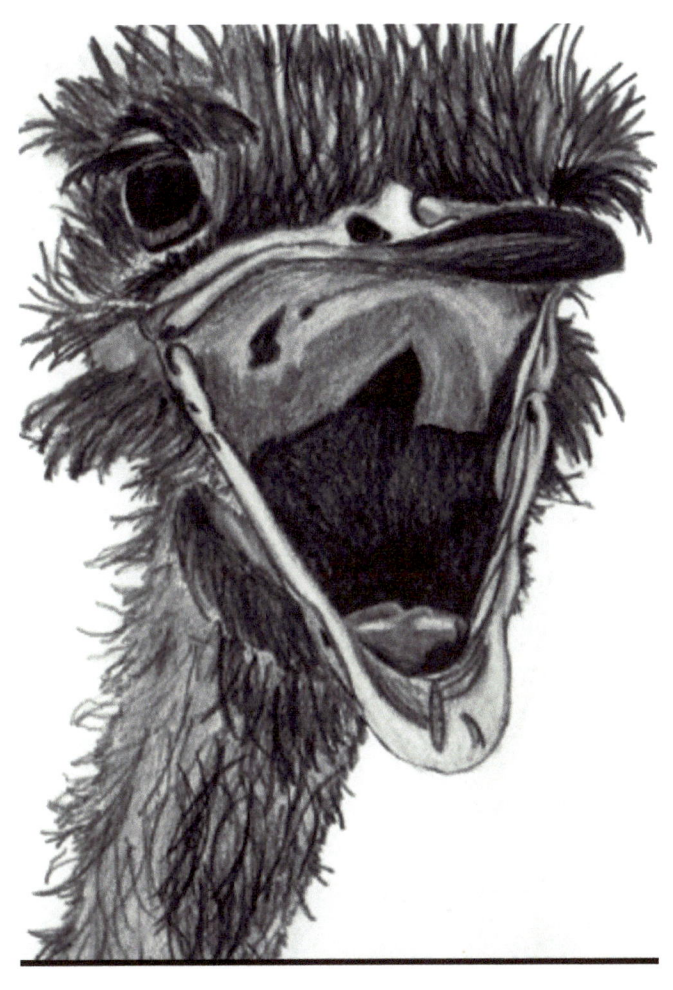

Ostrich, 1992

Pencil on Paper

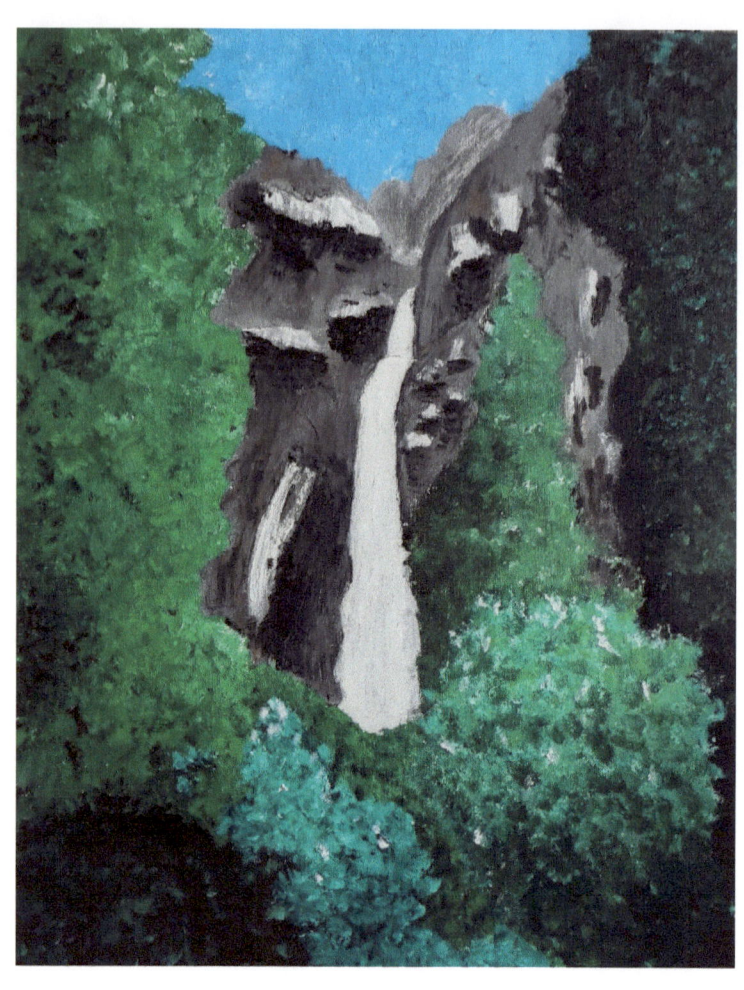

Waterfall, 1993

Acrylic Paint on Canvas

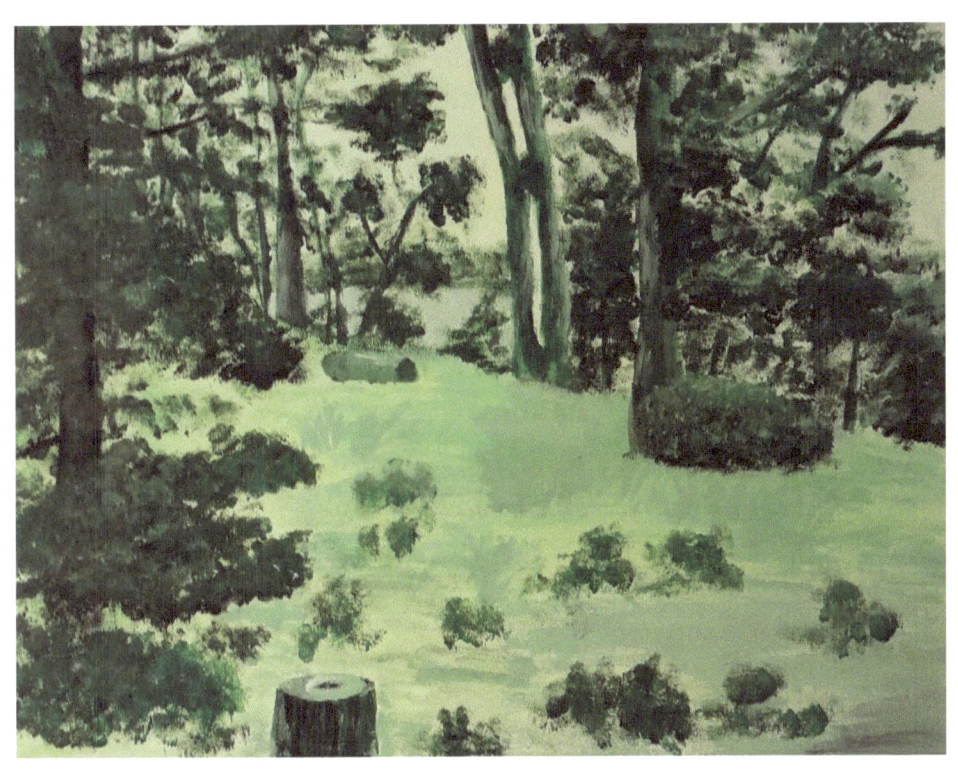

Silence, 1995

Acrylic Paint on Canvas

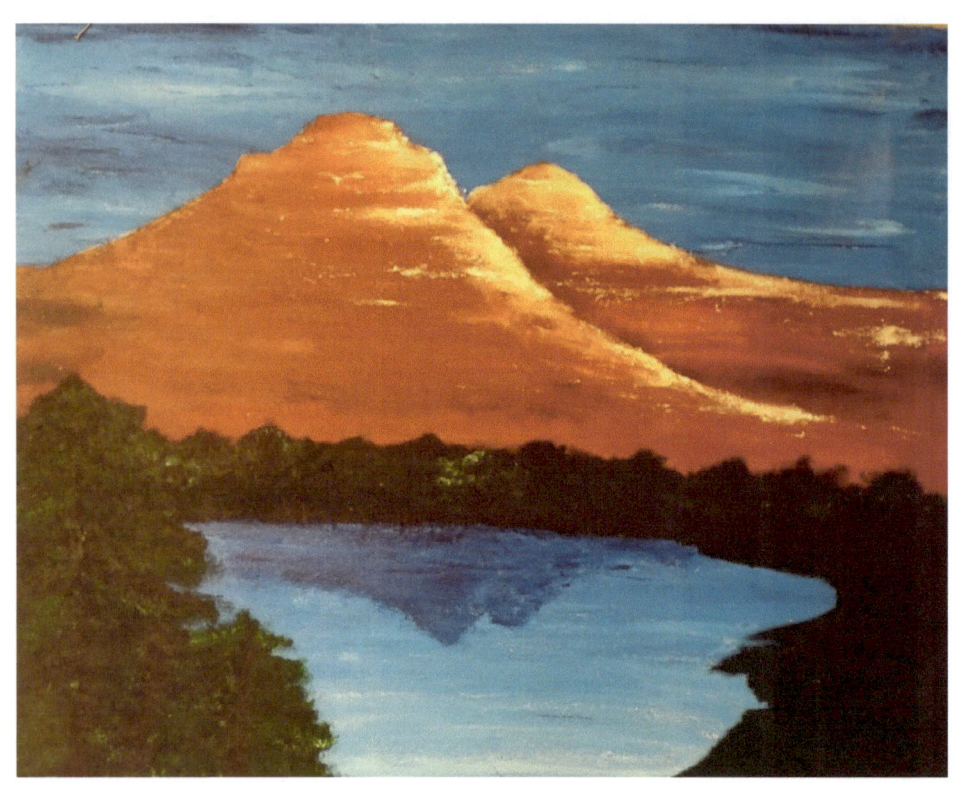

Red Mountains, 1996

Acrylic Paint on Canvas

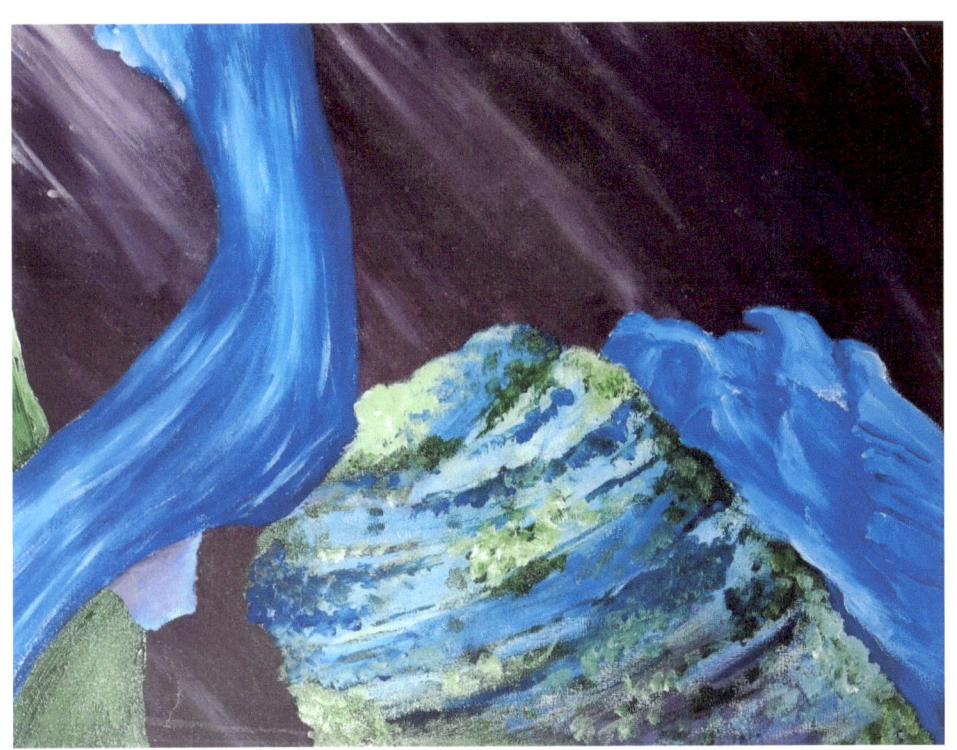

Blue, 1996

Acrylic Paint on Canvas

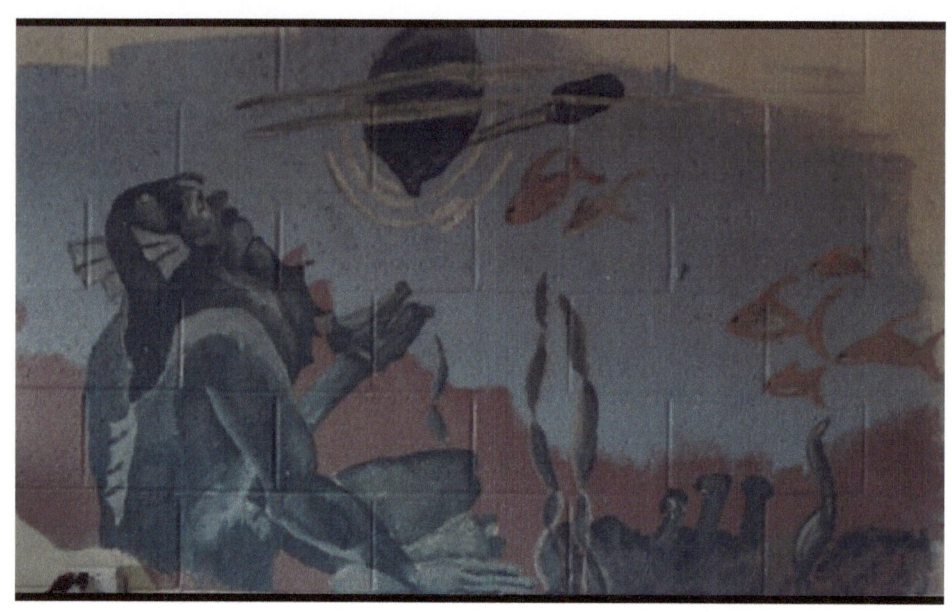

King Neptune, 1993

Wall Mural Paint

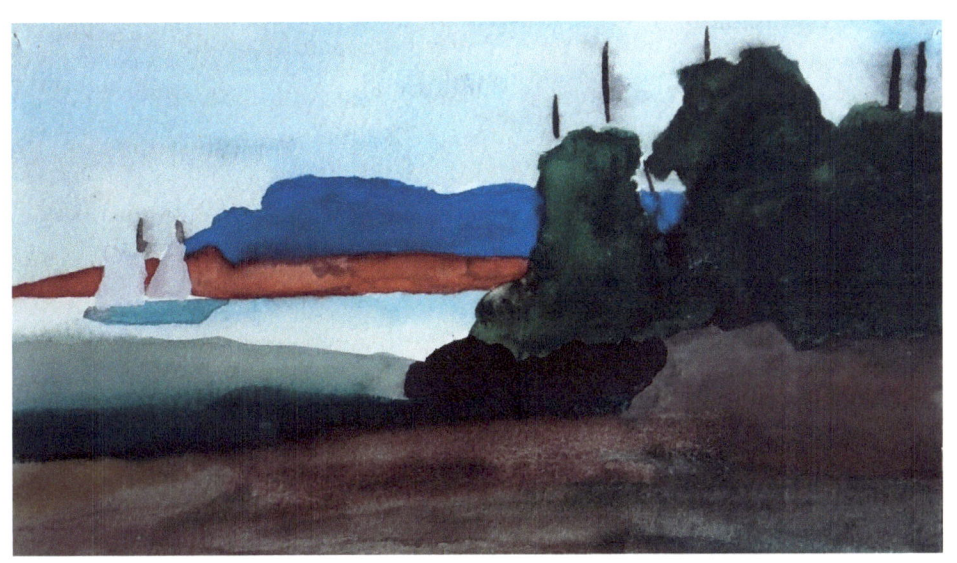

Serene, 1992

Watercolor Paint on Canvas

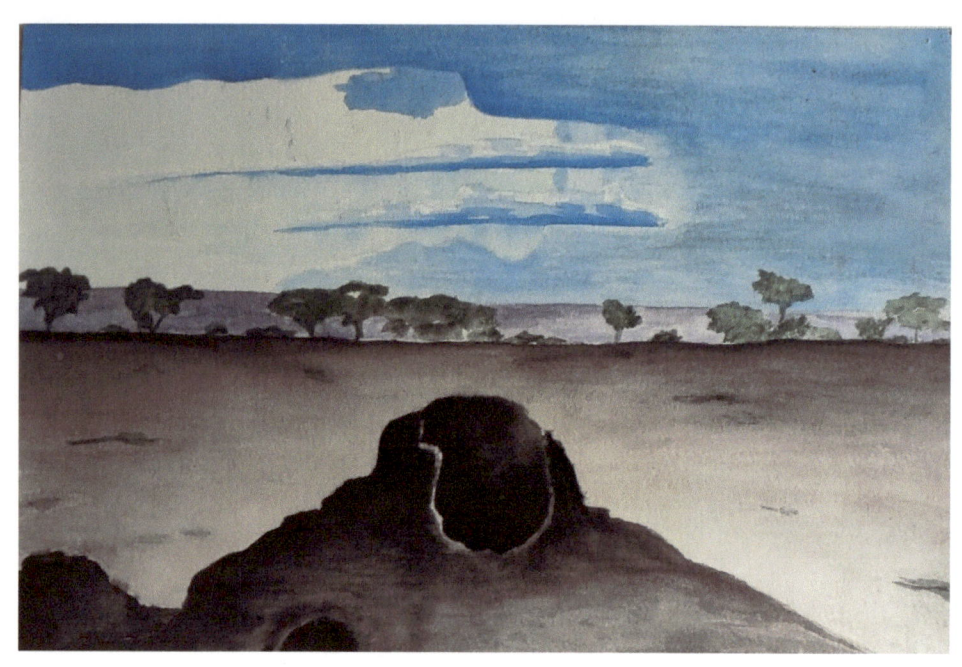

Outback, 1992

Watercolor Paint on Canvas

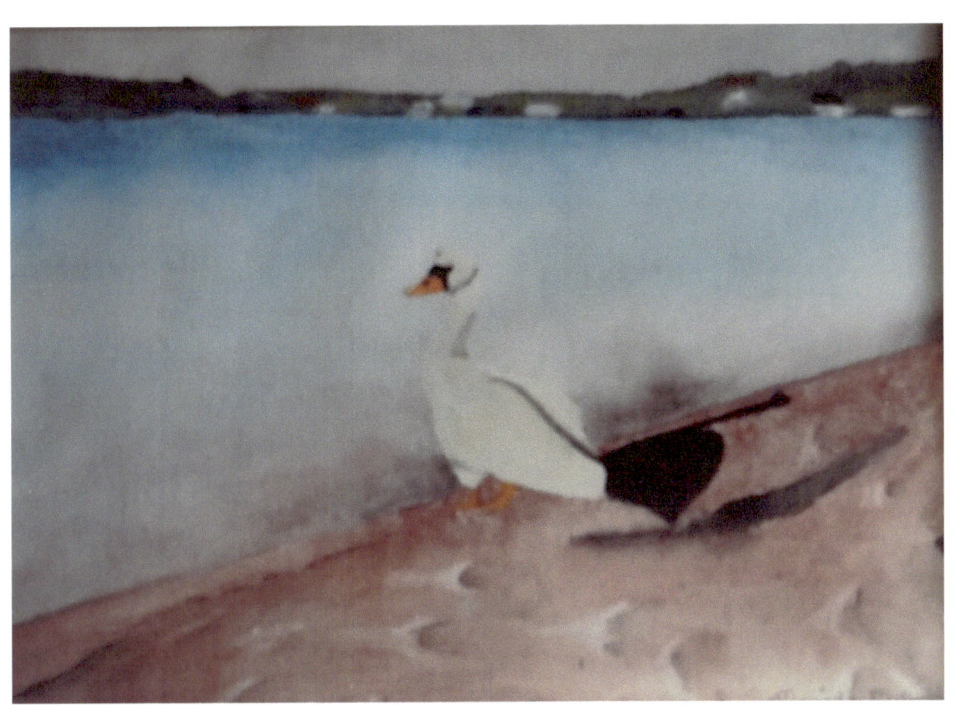

The Swan, 1991

Watercolor Paint on Canvas

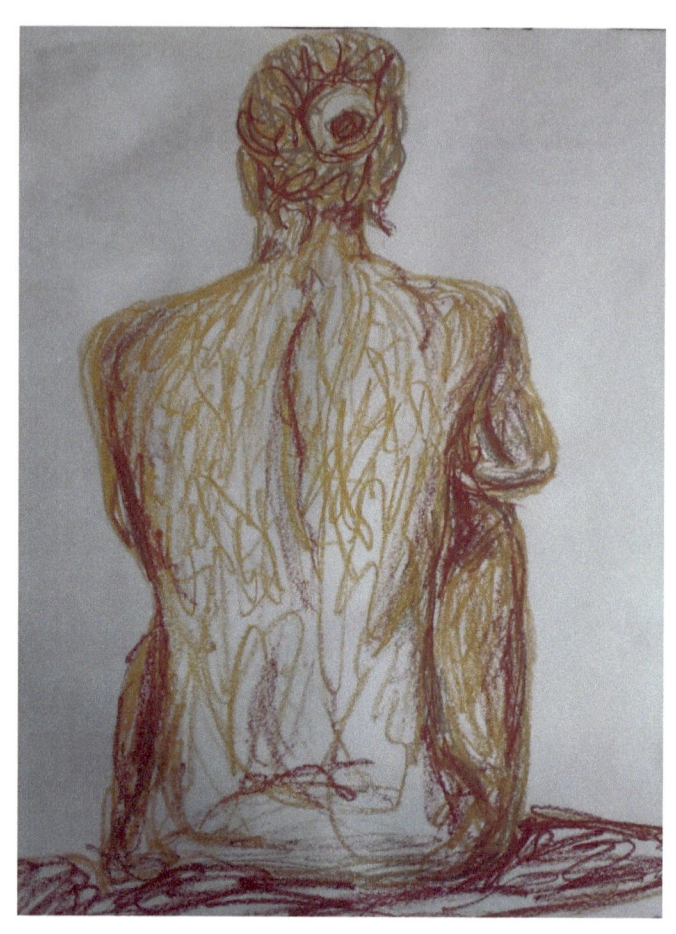

Orange Lady, 1996

Oil Pastel Stick on Paper

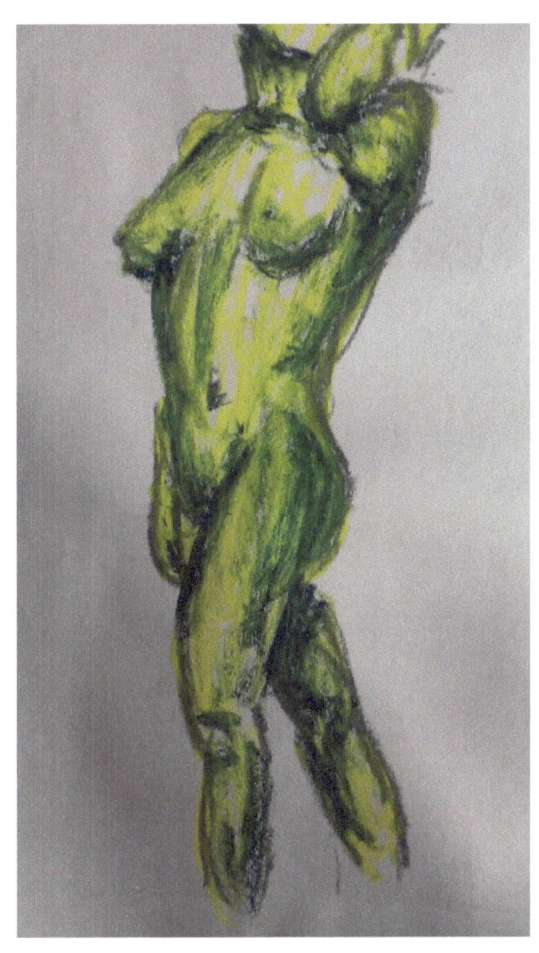

Yellow Woman, 1996

Oil Pastel Stick on Paper

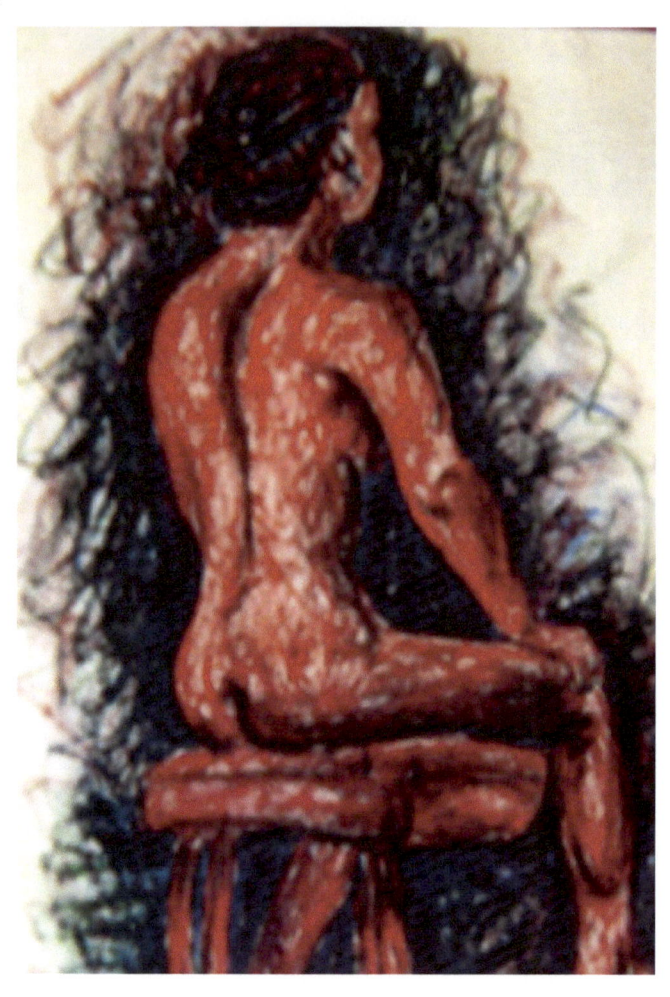

Red Lady, 1995

Oil Pastel Stick on Paper

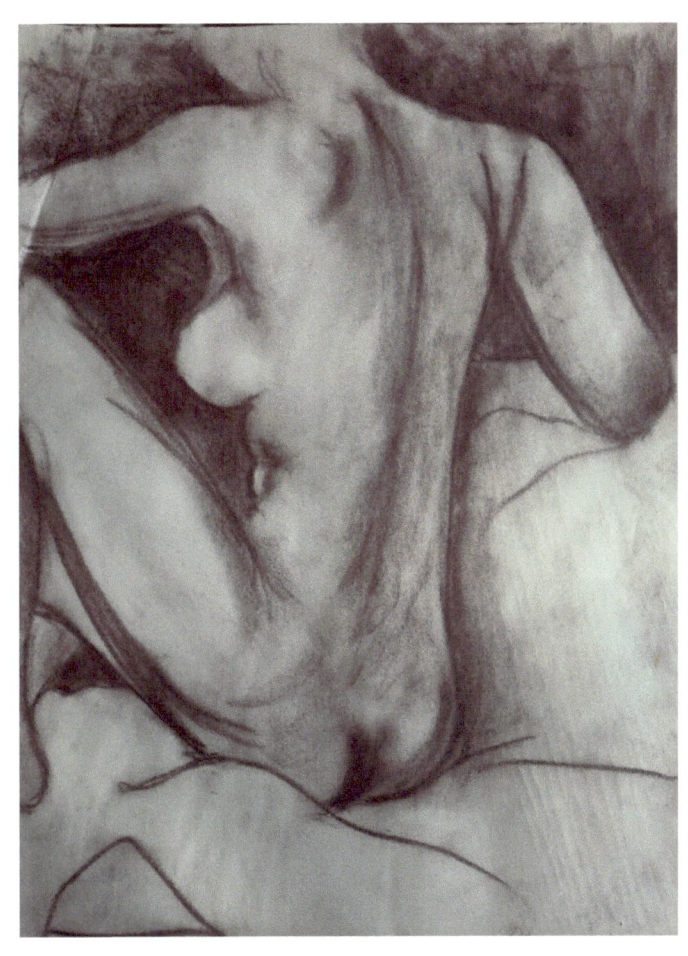

Sitting Woman, 1995

Charcoal on Paper

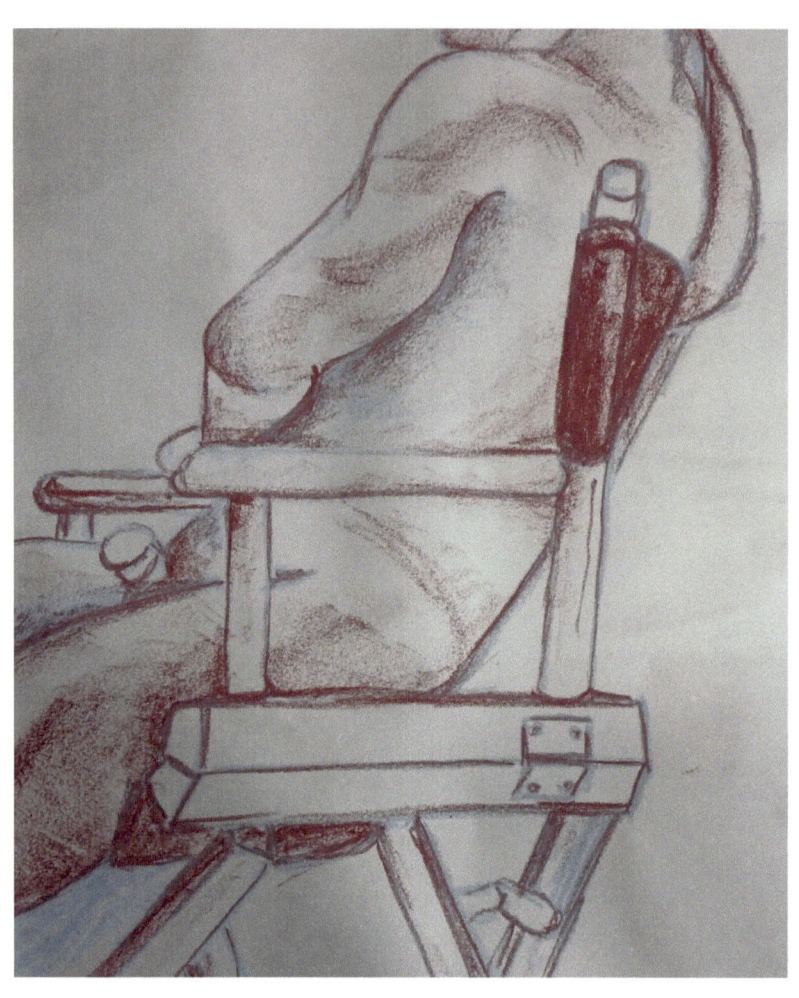

Sitting Man, 1995

Charcoal on Paper

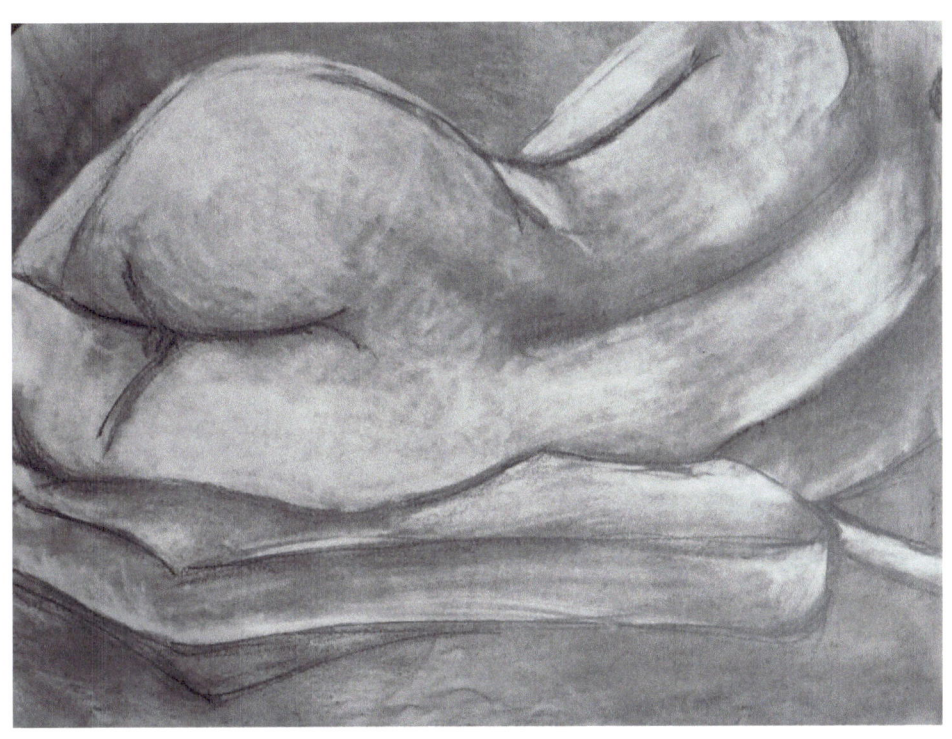

Laying Woman, 1994

Charcoal on Paper

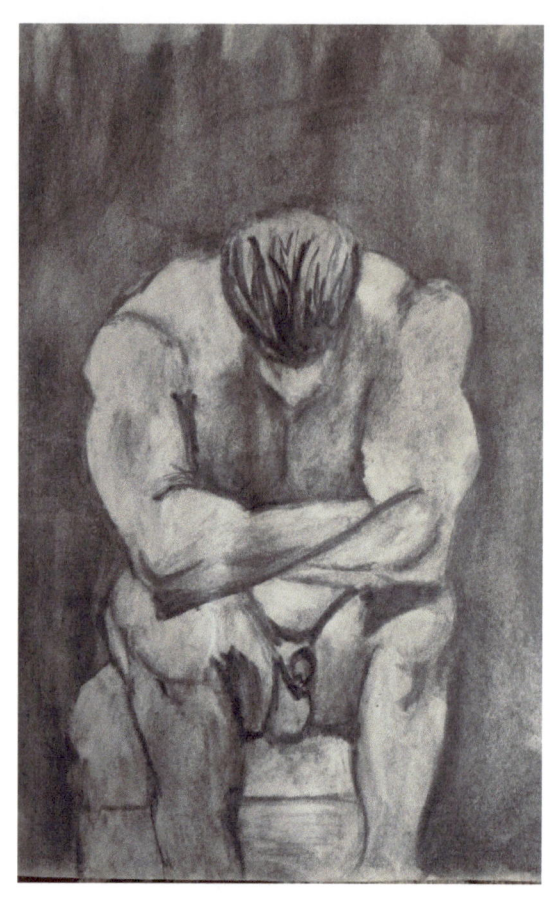

Man Contemplating, 1995

Graphite Stick on Paper

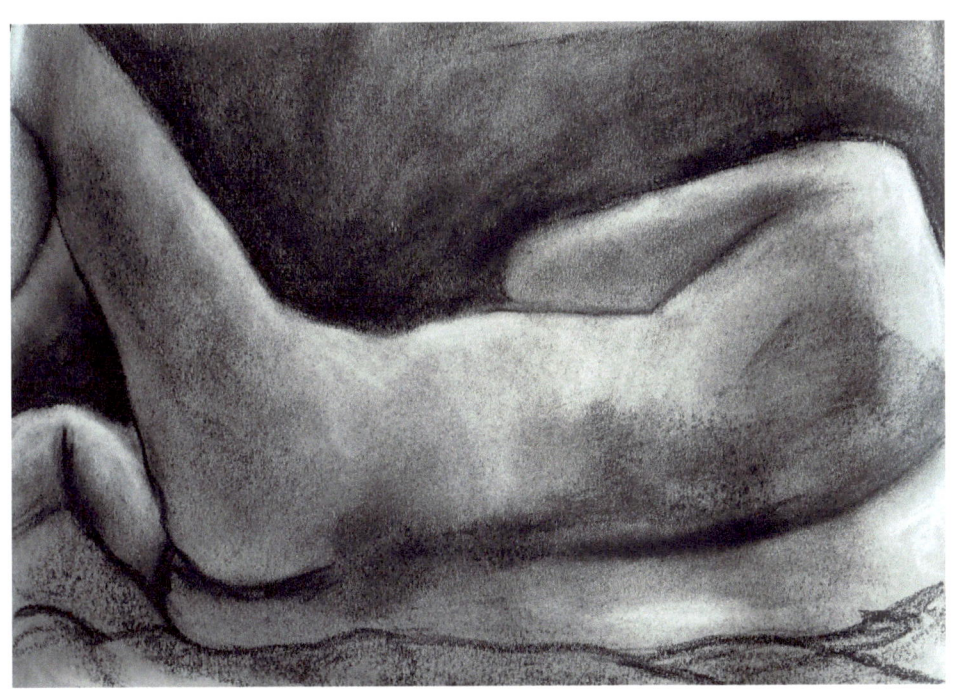

Man Laying, 1994

Charcoal on Paper

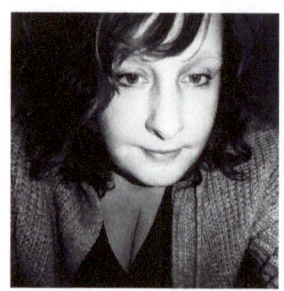

About the Artist

Artist M.D. LaBelle has been painting and drawing for over 35 years. She received a B.S. in Art from Central Michigan University in 2001 after transferring from Western Michigan University. M.D. LaBelle has experimented with a wide variety of mediums, but prefers oil pastel, acrylic and pencil. She lives in Michigan with her loving husband and four children at home.

M.D. LaBelle Paintings and Drawings

Copyright 2021 M.D. LaBelle

All Rights Reserved

All rights are reserved. No part of this publication may be reproduced, distributed or transmitted in any form or by any means, including photocopying, recording, or other electronic or mechanical methods, without the express prior written permission of the publisher, except in the case of brief quotations embodied in critical reviews and certain other noncommercial uses permitted by copyright law. For permission requests, please contact the artist through her email m.d.labelle0@gmail.com

www.ingramcontent.com/pod-product-compliance
Lightning Source LLC
Chambersburg PA
CBHW040451220526
45473CB00004B/1602